GENETICS

BY

JOANNA BRUNDLE

Published in 2020 by KidHaven Publishing, an Imprint of Greenhaven Publishing, LLC
353 3rd Avenue, Suite 255, New York, NY 10010

© 2020 Booklife Publishing

This edition is published by arrangement with Booklife Publishing.

Written by: Joanna Brundle
Edited by: Kirsty Holmes
Designed by: Drue Rintoul

Cataloging-in-Publication Data

Names: Brundle, Joanna.
Title: Genetics / Joanna Brundle.
Description: New York : KidHaven Publishing, 2020. | Series: Science in action | Includes glossary and index.
Identifiers: ISBN 9781534530881 (pbk.) | ISBN 9781534530171 (library bound) | ISBN 9781534531611 (6 pack) | ISBN 9781534530751 (ebook)
Subjects: LCSH: Genetics--Juvenile literature. | Genes--Juvenile literature. | DNA--Juvenile literature.
Classification: LCC QH437.5 B786 2020 | DDC 572.8--dc23

Photo credits
Abbreviations: l-left, r-right, b-bottom, t-top, c-center, m-middle.
Front Cover t – Konstantin Faraktinov. Front Cover mt – Marcin Balcerzak. Front Cover mb – Victoria Shapiro. Front Cover b – pixelheadphoto digitalskillet. 1. – ESB Professional. 2 – nobeastsofierce. 4tr – acceptphoto. 4bl – wong sze yuen. 5tr – By Geni (Photo by user:geni) [GFDL (http://www.gnu.org/copyleft/fdl.html) or CC BY-SA 4.0-3.0-2.5-2.0-1.0 (http://creativecommons.org/licenses/by-sa/4.0-3.0-2.5-2.0-1.0)], via Wikimedia Commons. 5bl – Kateryna Kon. 5br – donatas1205. 6tr – wavebreakmedia. 6bl – Alila Medical Media. 7tr – Rost9. 7br – Kateryna Kon. 8 – SARANS. 9tr – R Kristoffersen. 9bl – klss. 10 – Africa Studio. 11r – extender_01. 11br – Everett Historical. 13tr – Sebastian Kaulitzki. 13l – Morphart Creation. 13b – Craig Fraser. 14tr – Nicku. 14b – Jess Kraft. 15t – Peter Wey. 15b – ESB Professional. 16t – Rich Carey. 16b – Oldrich. 17tl – Timcharinee. 17mr – Anetlanda. 17b – By James L. Amos (National Geographic Society) [CC0], via Wikimedia Commons. 18tr – kentoh. 18b – Kateryna Kon. 19b – Belish. 20tr – MidoSemsem. 20br – Jagodka. 20bl – Dmitry Pichugin. 21tr – vvoe. 21l – Scisetti Alfio. 22 – all_about_people. 23 – Kateryna Kon. 24t – Valentyn Volkov. 24tr – John Wollwerth. 24tl – Alf Ribeiro. 24bl – Lynn2511. 24br – topseller. 25tr – Valentyn Volkov. 25b – Business Plus. 27t – Rob Hainer. 28tr – Couperfield. 29tr – Everett Historical. 29b – andersphoto. 30mr – Dudarev Mikhail. 30br – SOMRERK WITTHAYANANT. Images are courtesy of Shutterstock.com. With thanks to Getty Images, Thinkstock Photo and iStockphoto.

Printed in the United States of America

CPSIA compliance information: Batch #BS19KL: For further information contact Greenhaven Publishing LLC, New York, New York at 1-844-317-7404.

CONTENTS

Words that look like **this** are explained in the glossary on page 31.

WHAT IS GENETICS?

Have you ever heard people talking about genetically modified food, genetic testing, or designer babies? All these topics are about genetics. Genetics is something that affects us throughout our lives, even before we are born. New discoveries about genetics are being made all the time. But what is genetics and why does it matter?

GENES

Genetics is the scientific study of genes. Genes are like instruction manuals that tell living **organisms** how to work and grow. Genes are contained inside all living things. Our genes identify us as a particular type of organism.

Genes are found in cells – the tiny building blocks that make up all living things. The genes in the cells of this horse and foal give instructions about how a horse should develop. They give the horse its own **traits**, or characteristics, and they ensure that when a horse **reproduces**, it gives birth to a foal and not to a puppy! Genetic scientists study **heredity** – how characteristics are passed on from one **generation** to the next.

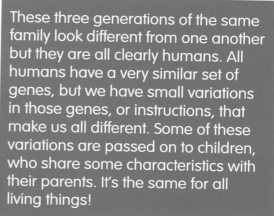

These three generations of the same family look different from one another but they are all clearly humans. All humans have a very similar set of genes, but we have small variations in those genes, or instructions, that make us all different. Some of these variations are passed on to children, who share some characteristics with their parents. It's the same for all living things!

4

THE RISE OF GENETICS

In the last sixty years, the study of genetics has moved way beyond understanding genes and heredity. Genetic scientists can now modify, or change, genes and create new types of plants and animals.

The genes in GM or genetically modified crops have been changed. GM crops may produce more food, they may be more **resistant** to disease and pests, they may stay fresh for longer, or they may contain more **nutrients**. Rice, for example, can be modified by including a gene from the daffodil plant. This type of rice contains extra vitamin A, needed for healthy eyes and bones. It can be grown in places where people's diet lacks this vitamin.

Genetic scientists are now able to produce copies of many plants and animals. This is called **cloning**. The copy produced is called a clone. Born in 1996, Dolly the sheep was the first **mammal** to be successfully cloned.

Cystic fibrosis, a disease which affects the lungs, is an example of a genetic disease. Genetic diseases can be passed on from parents to their children. Scientists have now perfected ways of checking cells for certain diseases before a baby starts to develop, so that the parents can have a healthy child.

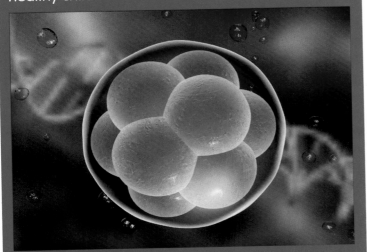

This tiny human **embryo** has only 16 cells, but it can still be tested for genetic diseases that could affect the baby that the embryo will become.

Genetic testing examines a person's genetic material. It can tell someone if they are in danger of becoming ill with certain diseases in the future. In some cases, a person can then reduce their risk. Someone who is genetically in danger of developing heart disease, for example, might decide to stop smoking, to eat healthily, or to get more exercise. Smoking, an unhealthy diet, and lack of exercise all make someone more likely to have heart disease.

CELLS, GENES, AND CHROMOSOMES

*You need a **microscope** to see cells. Although they are so small, they contain a huge amount of genetic information. Each cell has a nucleus, which is usually near the middle and looks like a round ball. The nucleus is the cell's command center. Genes are contained inside the nucleus and give the cell instructions.*

THE SAME BUT DIFFERENT

There are different types of cells in our bodies, for example skin or bone cells. These all work together to keep us healthy. Every cell nucleus has a copy of the same set of genes. In our bodies, each cell has a full set of around 30,000 genes. But each cell only uses the particular genes it needs to do its job. Some cells, for example, only use the genes that allow them to make keratin, a substance that is found in our hair and nails.

All humans have a full set of human genes, but small differences in our genes affect how we look, including the color of our eyes, skin, and hair and how tall we grow.

Typical Animal Cell

Nucleus Containing Genes and Chromosomes

DID YOU KNOW? SCIENTISTS ESTIMATE THAT THERE ARE 100 BILLION (THAT'S 1,000,000,000!) CELLS IN THE HUMAN BRAIN!

Cell Membrane (Outer Skin)

Every type of living thing has its own set of genes that make it look and grow differently from other living things. Genes are found on tiny structures called **chromosomes**.

CHROMOSOMES

Chromosomes look a bit like long, thin strands of spaghetti, but they often coil themselves up into X shapes (right).

There may be thousands of genes in just one chromosome. The genes are arranged in precise patterns. Chromosomes are usually found as matching pairs or sets of two. One half of each pair comes from the mother, while the other half of the pair comes from the father. Different living things have different numbers of pairs of chromosomes, but it remains a mystery why this is so. Humans have 23 pairs, or 46 altogether.

GIRL OR BOY?

Most of our chromosomes are the same whether we're male or female. But the shape of one of the chromosomes in the final pair is the key to whether we develop as a girl or a boy. In girls, both chromosomes in pair number 23 match and look like all other chromosomes. Boys have one X chromosome and one shorter one, called a Y chromosome.

E.coli Bacteria

Some simple organisms, such as E. coli bacteria and the male of some **species** of ant, have only one single chromosome. These organisms have no matching pairs of chromosomes.

DNA

DNA is the stuff that genes are made of. Chromosomes are long strands of DNA. The letters stand for deoxyribonucleic acid.

THE STRUCTURE OF DNA

DNA has a particular structure. Two strands of DNA spiral around one another to form a shape like a twisted ladder, called a double helix. DNA is made up of building blocks called nucleotides. These contain chemicals called bases. There are four bases: adenine, cytosine, guanine, and thymine. These are called A, C, G, and T – much easier to remember! Bases form pairs called base pairs. Each pair becomes one step on the DNA twisted ladder.

CRACKING THE CODE

Base pairs hold the twisted strands together. Notice the pattern of the bases. The same bases always pair up, A with T and C with G. The base pairs are arranged in many different combinations, to form a code. Cells act as code breakers and read these patterns of letters. The bases in genes are organized in sets of three, for example TGA or GGC. These genetic words are called codons. Sequences of codons act as an instruction manual for cells. Cells use substances called amino acids that we get from our food to make **proteins**. The patterns of codons tell the cells which amino acids to use and the order in which they should be joined together.

Base pairs

Double helix shape

DID YOU KNOW? WE SHARE 99.9% OF OUR DNA WITH EVERYONE ELSE ON EARTH. THE LAST 0.1% IS ENOUGH TO MAKE US ALL DIFFERENT – UNLESS WE ARE AN IDENTICAL TWIN. THEY HAVE ALMOST EXACTLY THE SAME DNA.

PROTEINS

Amino acids are the building blocks for proteins. Proteins are substances that make up or produce almost everything in our bodies. Some proteins form things like muscles and hair. Others make cells work. Insulin, for example, is a type of protein that helps us to digest sugars.

Each codon stands for a different amino acid. There are 20 amino acids altogether. Each protein has its own set of these building blocks, joined in a particular order. By reading the code, cells can make thousands of different proteins.

People with an illness called diabetes don't make enough insulin. They have to check the amount of sugar in their blood every day and inject extra insulin.

MAKING COPIES

As living things grow, cells divide or split into two new cells. That's how the tiny embryo shown on page 5 will eventually become a baby. When a cell divides, the DNA that it contains is able to make an exact copy of itself. This is called replication.

The two strands that make up the twisted ladder shape split, just like a zipper coming undone. Free bases in the cell that are not already paired up find a partner and eventually, two new identical DNA ladders are made. The two new cells have exactly the same DNA.

DID YOU KNOW? DNA IS THE ONLY **MOLECULE** FOUND IN LIVING THINGS THAT IS ABLE TO REPLICATE, OR MAKE AN EXACT COPY OF ITSELF.

HEREDITY

No living thing lives forever. All living things need to reproduce in order for their species to survive. Reproduction passes on genes from the parents to their young. This is why offspring look similar to their parents, but show some differences.

GENETIC TRAITS

Do you look like other people in your family? Have a look at some old photographs to see. Maybe you are a fast runner or are good at math – just like a parent or grandparent. Characteristics that are passed on from generation to generation are called genetic traits.

NATURE OR NURTURE

Although genes are important in making someone who they are, other things also play a big part. So, which do you think is more important, nature (genes) or nurture (the way we are brought up)?

Once we are born, factors such as the food we eat, the amount of exercise we get, and the type of education we receive all affect how we grow up. Our families and friends may influence our behavior and the choices we make. But it is important to remember that only genetic traits are inherited.

This young ballerina has inherited traits that may help her as a dancer. But, even with this advantage, she will still have to practice hard if she wants to be successful. Nature and nurture must work together.

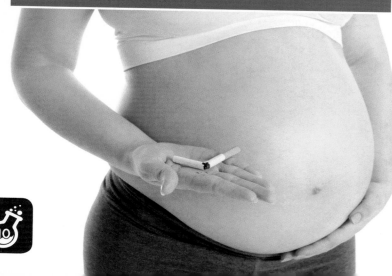

If a mother smokes while she is pregnant, her baby is twice as likely to be born too soon and to have a low birth weight. Nurture affects us, even before we are born.

DOMINANT GENES

As we have seen, our genes come from both our parents. Genes that control particular features such as our eye color can come in different versions called **alleles**. The allele for brown eyes is called a dominant gene because it will always win in terms of deciding what color eyes we have.

BLUE OR BROWN EYES?

GENE FROM DAD	CHILD'S EYE COLOR	GENE FROM MOM
(brown eye)	(brown eye)	(brown eye)
(brown eye)	(brown eye)	(blue eye)
(blue eye)	(brown eye)	(brown eye)
(blue eye)	(blue eye)	(blue eye)

RECESSIVE GENES

The gene that is beaten by the dominant gene is called the recessive gene. The gene or allele for blue eyes is a recessive gene. Recessive genes can cause some serious illnesses like sickle cell disease. If a child suffers from this type of disease, they have inherited the recessive gene from both parents.

Normal Red Blood Cell

Curved, Sickle-Shaped Cell

People who suffer from sickle cell disease have some curved or sickle-shaped red blood cells. These cells can block blood vessels, causing breathing difficulties and muscle cramps.

MUTATIONS

Mutations are tiny changes to the coded instructions in DNA. They can happen if cells don't copy one another exactly when they divide. Mutations may be harmless, but sometimes they cause problems. The serious illness called hemophilia, which stops blood from clotting, is caused by a mutation.

The son of Tsar Nicholas ll of Russia, Tsarevich Alexei, famously suffered from hemophilia.

The Russian Royal Family, 1914

BABY TALK

A boy and a girl share many characteristics. They both have a brain, and two eyes and ears, for example. But they have different reproductive organs, which are the parts of the body that will eventually enable them to have their own children.

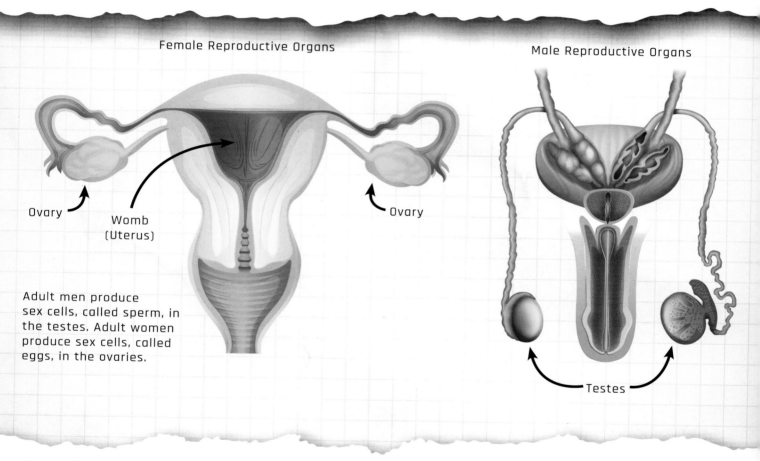

Female Reproductive Organs

Ovary

Womb
(Uterus)

Ovary

Adult men produce sex cells, called sperm, in the testes. Adult women produce sex cells, called eggs, in the ovaries.

Male Reproductive Organs

Testes

Sex cells are different from normal cells because they have only 23 chromosomes – half the usual number. If a sperm joins with an egg, the egg is said to be fertilized. The nucleus of the sperm joins with the nucleus of the egg to give a full set of 46 chromosomes. A fertilized egg can begin to grow inside the womb, or uterus, of the mother.

So, how does a baby form from this one fertilized egg? The cell divides into two and these cells divide again. The process continues. Each new cell carries the complete set of genes which give instructions for making a baby. After only a few days, some cells follow particular instructions and begin to form various body parts.

As the embryo grows and begins to look more like a baby, it is known as a **fetus**.

After around nine months, a human baby is ready to be born. One fertilized egg cell has become around 200 million cells! After birth, instructions from the genes tell the body how to continue to grow and develop. Throughout our lives, genetic instructions make our bodies work and produce the new cells and substances needed to stay alive.

At 20 weeks, the ears, eyes, nose, fingers, and toes can all be recognized.

Anne Boleyn, second wife of King Henry VIII

Sometimes, a mutation or genetic fault can happen while a fetus is growing. Some people say Anne Boleyn had six fingers on her right hand! This would have been a result of a mutation.

GESTATION

Gestation is the time between fertilization of an egg and the birth of the young. How long the gestation period lasts varies a great deal between different creatures. Mice are born after just 21 days, but the gestation period for African elephants is almost two years!

Giraffes are pregnant for an average of 430 days. Like human babies, giraffes begin as a single fertilized egg but their different genes mean that they develop their own special characteristics.

EVOLUTION

There are millions of different species of living things, but they all came about because of a process called evolution. Evolution is the very gradual change in the characteristics of a species over many generations. The English scientist Charles Darwin was the first person to study and explain evolution.

DARWIN'S DISCOVERIES

In 1831, Darwin began a round-the-world voyage on board the HMS *Beagle*. While visiting the Galápagos Islands in the Pacific Ocean, he noticed that many species on the islands were found there and nowhere else. Darwin thought that these species had originally come from nearby South America. He concluded that, over millions of years, they had gradually changed or **adapted** to suit their new **environment**, until they no longer resembled their South American relatives.

Charles Darwin (1809-1882)

The Galápagos flightless cormorant has no natural enemies. It does not need to be able to fly away and so, over time, has evolved into a flightless bird.

Darwin noticed that members of the same species show natural differences or variations. He thought that these variations would make some better able than others to compete for food, water, and shelter. These creatures, he believed, were much more likely to survive and thus pass on their useful characteristics to their young. This process is called natural selection. It is sometimes called survival of the fittest. Over time, the creatures that survive are those best adapted to their environment.

White rabbits are adapted to living in snowy conditions because they are camouflaged to hide them from **predators**. Darwin's theory suggests that white rabbits have evolved from brown rabbits. White rabbits would be much more likely to survive and reproduce than brown rabbits, which are not camouflaged in snow.

EVOLUTION AND DNA

Using their knowledge of DNA and how accidental changes in DNA cause mutations, scientists now believe that all living things, including humans, evolved from one common **ancestor** that lived billions of years ago. Evolution over millions of generations has produced the huge number and variety of species now living on Earth.

Next time you sit down to dinner, remember that you and all the vegetables, fruit, fish, or animals that you may be eating may have evolved from one common ancestor. You're all related!

EXTINCTION

A species becomes extinct when there are no longer any living members of that species. Extinction is the process by which this happens. Extinction can be caused by many things, including changes in climate or the destruction of a species' natural **habitat.** *The actions of humans are often to blame.*

Deforestation of tropical rain forests has led to the extinction of many species. Many are currently in danger, including the mountain gorilla and the orangutan.

DID YOU KNOW?
CLONING MIGHT BE A WAY TO SAVE **ENDANGERED SPECIES** LIKE THE RHINOCEROS. SOME SCIENTISTS ALSO THINK THAT IT MIGHT EVENTUALLY BE POSSIBLE TO USE DNA TO BRING BACK SPECIES THAT ARE ALREADY EXTINCT.

Extinction can also be caused by diseases, other species competing for food, or new predators – including humans.

The horn of the rhinoceros is very valuable. The rhinoceros has been hunted by humans for its horn, almost to the point of extinction.

The simple answer to this question is **biodiversity**. Biodiversity is the word used for the wide range of different species in the world. Biodiversity is very important to life on Earth. Around 80% of all our medicines, for example, are obtained from natural sources. New ones are being discovered all the time. The loss of different species makes it less likely that this will happen in the future.

The rosy periwinkle, a flowering plant found in Madagascar, is now used to make drugs that fight **cancer**.

FOSSILS

Fossils are the preserved remains of plants or animals. Fossils form when an organism is buried, often by sand or mud, soon after it dies. In a gradual process that usually takes millions of years, the plant and animal tissue is gradually replaced by minerals. The surrounding mud and sand turn to rock.

Some fossils are the preserved traces of an animal, such as its droppings or its footprints. Many small creatures, like this scorpion, have been fossilized in amber. Amber is the hardened sap from a prehistoric pine tree. Some fossils have been preserved in ice or wet, boggy areas called peat bogs.

This fossil of a creature called an *Archaeopteryx* shares characteristics with dinosaurs and birds. It represents one tiny step on the journey of evolution.

FOSSILS AND EVOLUTION

Paleontologists are scientists who study fossils. They use various techniques and equipment, including scanners and X-ray cameras, to find out about the diet, lifestyle, and growth of the fossilized animal or plant. The **fossil record** is also strong evidence to support Darwin's evolution theory. Many fossilized birds, for example, have teeth, even though no living species of bird has teeth. How can this be? Birds evolved from dinosaurs that did have teeth. Over millions of years, birds lost their teeth because they were not needed.

THE HUMAN GENOME

A genome is a complete set of the genes found in an organism. The human genome is made up of all the DNA in one of the two sets of chromosomes from 1 to 22 and both of the sex chromosomes. That makes 24 altogether.

THE HUMAN GENOME PROJECT

The Human Genome Project was set up in 1990. Its purpose was to map or work out the order of all the bases (see page 8) that make up the coded messages, or instructions, in our genes.

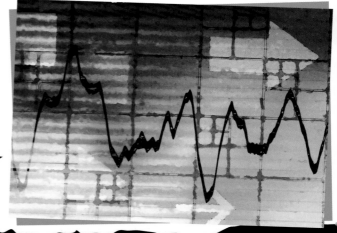

This computer image shows a map of some human DNA.

The project was also set up to work out the position on our chromosomes of all the different genes that make up a human being. It proved to be a very difficult task! Thousands of scientists in six different countries (France, Germany, Japan, China, the U.S., and the U.K.) took part. Cells used in the project were donated by volunteers. To help them make sense of the human genome, scientists also looked at the genome of simple organisms like the roundworm.

Although a roundworm is only 0.04 inch (1 mm) long, its genome has 97 million base pairs (see page 8).

HUMAN GENOME PROJECT DISCOVERIES

The project took 13 years to complete. Scientists found out that the human genome has 3,200 million base pairs. No wonder it took so long! The project also discovered that around 30,000 genes make up the human genome. This was a lot less than the 100,000 that scientists had predicted.

DID YOU KNOW? STRETCHED OUT AND JOINED TOGETHER, THERE IS ABOUT 6.5 FEET (2 M) OF DNA IN EVERY CELL. ONLY A TINY PERCENTAGE OF OUR DNA (AROUND THREE PERCENT) IS MADE UP OF GENES. THE REST IS MADE UP OF BASE PAIRS (SEE PAGE 8) IN RANDOM PATTERNS. IT'S CALLED JUNK DNA.

THE IMPORTANCE OF THE HUMAN GENOME PROJECT

The information obtained from the project has helped scientists to develop new ways of curing, treating, and preventing human diseases. There are now, for example, thousands of genetic tests that can be carried out on patients to see if they already have an illness or are in danger of developing it. The causes of extremely rare diseases can be understood.

A baby cannot speak for itself and tell a doctor about its pain or symptoms. Progress that has been made as a result of the project means that a child's genome can now be known quickly. This can save a child's life because the right treatment can be given promptly. Eventually, the genome of all babies may be recorded shortly after birth, by analyzing a blood sample.

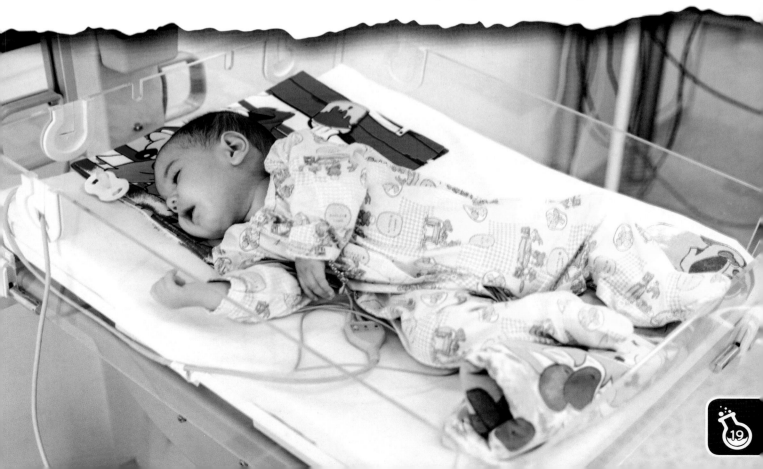

EARLY DISCOVERIES

Since the earliest civilizations, people have noticed that offspring share traits or characteristics with their parents. The ancient Greek thinker Aristotle (384-322 BC) suggested that organisms develop from miniature versions of themselves. He thought, for example, that a male human parent provided a complete mini human, which then developed inside the female parent's body.

Aristotle also thought traits were passed on in blood, which may be why we still use expressions like "blood relatives" or "bloodline." The fact that some diseases seem to run in families was noticed by early Hindus, 2,000 years ago.

Aristotle

SELECTIVE BREEDING

For thousands of years, people have been using genetics to breed plants and animals with useful characteristics. This process is called selective breeding.

Prehistoric Cave Painting Showing Early Man with Cattle

Man has been selectively breeding cattle for centuries.

Farmers today still deliberately choose the strongest, biggest, and healthiest animals and plants for breeding. This increases the amount and quality of the food produced.

Dogs that are entered in competitions have been selectively bred to have special characteristics that judges are looking for. This Lhasa Apso has been bred to have a desirable solid shape and heavy coat.

GREGOR MENDEL

Mendel (1822-1884) was an Austrian monk who is known as the father of modern genetics. From 1856 to 1863, he carried out experiments, using pea plants grown in the monastery gardens.

This is the monastery in the Czech Republic where Mendel worked.

Mendel chose pea plants for his experiments because they reproduce quickly and show clear characteristics, such as height and flower color.

MENDEL'S FACTORS

Pea plants can have white or purple flowers. Mendel crossbred purple flowering plants with white flowering plants. All the offspring plants had purple flowers. He repeated his experiments with tall and short plants. All the offspring plants were tall. Mendel concluded that there was something, which he called factors, in the parent plants that affected the characteristics of the offspring. Mendel worked out that the factor for purple flowers or for tallness always won. The factor for white flowers or shortness always lost. Mendel had discovered the dominant and recessive genes that we looked at on page 11.

DID YOU KNOW? MENDEL'S EXPERIMENTS WERE IGNORED FOR MANY YEARS. THE DEVELOPMENT OF POWERFUL MICROSCOPES AT THE END OF THE 19TH CENTURY ALLOWED SCIENTISTS TO SEE CHROMOSOMES. MENDEL'S IDEAS HAD BEEN RIGHT ALL ALONG! HIS "FACTORS" WERE RENAMED "GENES."

GENETIC
ENGINEERING

Genetic engineering is the term used for the process in which scientists alter an organism's genes to give it different characteristics. Scientists genetically modify something by changing, removing, or adding to its DNA. Genetic engineering is used in many ways— for example to make new medicines, new materials, and genetically modified foods.

MEDICINES

If we cut ourselves or have a nosebleed, the bleeding eventually stops because a substance in our bodies called factor VIII makes blood go thick and sticky, or clot. People suffering from hemophilia don't make this substance naturally. It can now be made using genetic engineering techniques. The factor VIII gene from a healthy person can be introduced into nonhuman cells, such as the kidney cells of a baby hamster. The gene carries instructions for the hamster cell about how to make factor VIII – a bit like a recipe book. The hamster cells produce factor VIII, which can then be collected and injected into patients. Other common substances, such as insulin and albumin, which is used to treat burns, are now made in similar ways.

CANCER

Cancer is a very serious disease. The cells in our bodies are constantly being replaced. Normally, this happens in a controlled way. Cancer happens when cells in the body divide and grow in an uncontrolled way. This is usually caused by mutations or mistakes in a person's genes. Traditional treatments for cancer such as chemotherapy are very unpleasant for the patient. Scientists are developing many new treatments that involve making changes to the patient's DNA so that the faulty gene can be corrected.

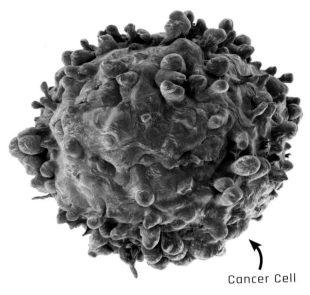

Cancer Cell

GOOD OR EVIL?

Some people believe that genetic engineering is wrong. Some believe that swapping genes could cause serious problems for our health and our environment in ways that we don't yet understand. Some religious groups accuse scientists of "playing God." They think that only God should be able to create or modify living things. Biodiversity (see page 16) could also be affected. Genetically modified crops, for example, could lead to a similar but nonmodified crop being wiped out, because it is less able to survive.

Anthrax is a deadly bacteria that causes breathing difficulties if it enters the body. It can be used as a **biological weapon**. Some people think that anthrax and other bacteria could be made even more dangerous by genetic engineering.

GENETICALLY MODIFIED (GM) FOODS

*Millions of people around the world are starving. There are many reasons why **famine** happens. Often, it is because crops fail, due to lack of water or damage from pests. Genetic engineering can help to prevent famine by genetically modifying crops so that they can survive in dry conditions or by becoming resistant to pests.*

Corn can be genetically modified to be resistant to pests like this corn borer.

This corn crop has died due to lack of water.

It is estimated that around a third of all the food produced in the world goes to waste. This is partly because it decays or rots before it can be eaten. Genetic engineering can produce crops that are resistant to mold. Scientists have even tried to produce a tomato that can't be destroyed by frost. This kind of tomato would contain an antifreeze gene, transferred from a fish called the flounder. It lives in very cold water and has a gene to keep it from freezing to death. The GM tomato wouldn't smell or taste fishy! Food that stays fresh for longer could reduce waste.

The pepper on the right has been grown on a plant that was genetically modified to be resistant to mold.

SAFE OR NOT?

GM foods have to be carefully tested before they can be sold, to make sure that they are safe for us to eat. Most of us will already have eaten GM foods, probably without even realizing it.

This isn't a real orange! GM foods don't look strange. In fact, they look exactly like normal food and you wouldn't be able to tell the difference just by looking.

Despite all the tests that have been carried out, some people still fear that growing GM crops could damage us and our environment. They argue that harmless butterflies and insects could be wiped out by crops that have been modified to make them poisonous to pests. We are all part of a huge **food chain** and interfering with it could cause problems for other species. Many countries ban the growing of GM crops – but they still import them from other countries.

Some people feel so strongly about GM foods that they choose to attend protest marches. Others risk being arrested for entering farmland illegally and destroying GM crops.

GENETIC TESTING

Genetic testing is used to work out if a patient has faults or mutations in their genes. The results of genetic tests can tell someone how likely they are either to have a genetic disease in the future or to pass it on to their children.

ALZHEIMER'S DISEASE

Alzheimer's disease affects the brain and causes memory and speech problems. It is affecting more and more older people. A test has now been developed that can tell the age at which someone might get the disease. Although there is no cure, drugs that slow it down work well, if they are taken at an early stage. Genetic testing can tell someone when they will need treatment.

DID YOU KNOW? GENETIC TESTING COULD BE USED AGAINST YOU. PEOPLE AT RISK OF DEVELOPING SERIOUS ILLNESSES COULD FIND IT HARD TO GET A JOB OR **LIFE INSURANCE**. MANY COUNTRIES HAVE LAWS TO PROTECT PRIVATE GENETIC INFORMATION FOR THIS REASON.

Thick, sticky mucus blocks airways.

Cystic fibrosis is caused by a genetic mistake in chromosome number seven.

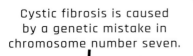

CYSTIC FIBROSIS

Cystic fibrosis is a genetic disease. The faulty gene in cystic fibrosis patients makes sticky mucus build up in the lungs. The mucus causes breathing difficulties.

A baby will only inherit the disease if both parents pass on a copy of the faulty gene. A genetic test can help the parents to have a healthy baby. Eggs from the mother are fertilized with sperm from the father in a **laboratory**. The embryos that develop are tested for the faulty gene. Two or three healthy embryos are then implanted into the mother and may grow into babies.

DESIGNER BABIES

Designer babies are babies that develop from embryos that have been chosen for their healthy genes. Genetic testing of human embryos can also show whether the child will be a boy or a girl. This can be a good thing. The genetic disease called Duchenne muscular dystrophy, for example, affects only boys. Parents in a family affected by this disease can have a healthy child and avoid passing the condition on by having only girls. But it could also be a bad thing. In some cultures, boys are much more highly valued than girls, so parents might deliberately choose not to have girl babies, upsetting the natural balance of boys and girls. One day, people might be able to choose characteristics for their children, such as good looks or intelligence. Do you think this would be a good thing for the human race?

GENE THERAPY

Gene therapy works by identifying a faulty gene that is causing a disease and replacing it with a healthy gene. It's a bit like an engineer replacing a faulty part on a washing machine or computer! Gene therapy is still very new but it has already been used to treat some diseases, such as **hereditary** blindness. Here's how it works:

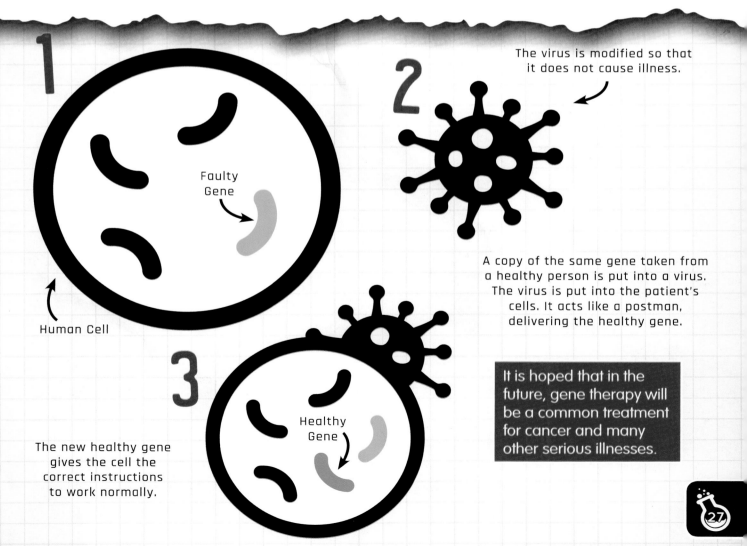

1

Human Cell

Faulty Gene

2

The virus is modified so that it does not cause illness.

A copy of the same gene taken from a healthy person is put into a virus. The virus is put into the patient's cells. It acts like a postman, delivering the healthy gene.

3

Healthy Gene

The new healthy gene gives the cell the correct instructions to work normally.

It is hoped that in the future, gene therapy will be a common treatment for cancer and many other serious illnesses.

DNA FINGERPRINTING

Everyone has their own special DNA pattern. It's what makes us all different. For this reason, looking at someone's DNA is a very precise way of working out who they are. Because a person's DNA is individual, just like their fingerprints, the process is called DNA fingerprinting. It's useful in many ways.

DNA EVIDENCE

The police can use DNA fingerprinting to arrest and convict criminals. They can also use it to rule innocent people out of their investigations. DNA collected at crime scenes is compared to the DNA of people the police think may have carried out a crime. If there is a match, the police have found the criminal.

Forensic scientists gather and then study evidence found at crime scenes.

A single hair, a flake of skin, or a drop of saliva or blood can give enough DNA to identify someone who may have been at a crime scene. Small sections of DNA are transferred to a special gel. Everyone's DNA forms different patterns in the gel. Special equipment then looks at the patterns and produces an image of the DNA that looks a bit like a barcode.

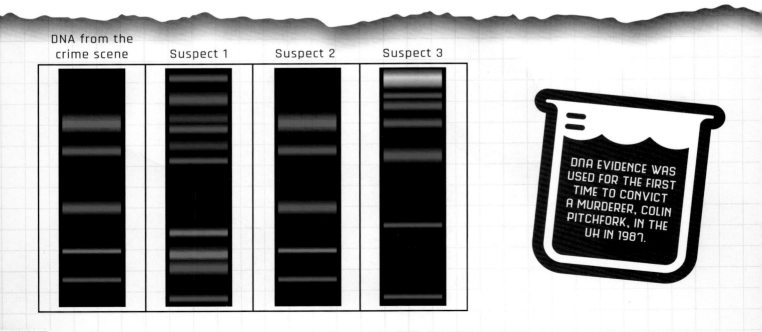

DNA from the crime scene Suspect 1 Suspect 2 Suspect 3

DNA EVIDENCE WAS USED FOR THE FIRST TIME TO CONVICT A MURDERER, COLIN PITCHFORK, IN THE UK IN 1987.

Look closely. Which suspect's DNA matches the crime scene DNA? Which suspect do you think is guilty?

FAMILY CONNECTIONS

Families can be split up for many reasons. Sometimes, parents are not able to look after their children, who then have to be adopted. Wars and natural disasters such as earthquakes can also cause family members to be separated from one another. DNA fingerprinting can help people to find out the identities of their birth parents and other relatives. DNA **databases** hold information about people who are looking for members of their family and can help to reunite them. During World War II, for example, many Jewish people were removed from their homes and killed in the **Holocaust**. Some survived, however, and DNA evidence has been used to track down members of the same family.

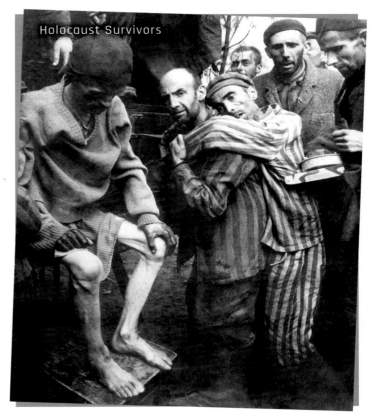

Holocaust Survivors

During World War II, many Jews were sent to camps, called concentration camps, where most were killed.

DNA AND ARCHAEOLOGY

Archaeologists are historians who study the remains of people and things. Where DNA samples still exist, scientists can work out the age of remains by comparing this DNA with modern-day samples. In 2015, archaeologists discovered a fossil tooth from an extinct species of human. The DNA it still contained helped them to work out that it was 110,000 years old!

Mummy

MANY PEOPLE WHO WERE CONVICTED OF CRIMES THEY DIDN'T COMMIT AND WHO WERE WRONGLY SENT TO PRISON HAVE BEEN FREED IN RECENT YEARS, THANKS TO DNA EVIDENCE.

Mummifying bodies, a process used by the Egyptians and Romans, preserves DNA in teeth, bones, and body tissues.

WHAT DO YOU THINK?

Genetics raises some important questions. Talk about some of the following ideas with your friends and family. Listen to other people's ideas.

GM CROPS

Genetically modified food crops could help to feed starving people around the world. Does that mean we should allow them to be grown everywhere? Would people who protest against them feel differently if they were starving? Should we really be thinking about how to stop wasting food and how to share it fairly around the world?

GM ANIMALS

Some animals are genetically modified to help humans. Useful medicines can be obtained from the milk of GM cows, for example. Is it right to use animals in this way?

GENETIC SCREENING

One day, we may be able to test human embryos for all genetic human diseases so that all inherited disease can be wiped out. Would it be a good thing to create "perfect" humans? Should we value our differences and disabilities?

CLONING

Cloning of human beings might become a reality. It could help childless people to have a family. Do you believe it is up to a higher power to create human life or should we be able to decide for ourselves?

LIVING LONGER

Genetic engineering could eventually alter our DNA so that we live much longer. It might be a good thing, but only if we stayed healthy. But many parts of the world are already overcrowded and don't have enough food or water. So would it be fair?

GLOSSARY

adapted   altered or modified to suit a particular environment

alleles   different forms of the same gene

ancestor   a relative, usually one generation further back in time than a grandparent

biodiversity   the variety of plant and animal life in the world or in a particular habitat

biological weapons   poisons or deadly diseases intended to kill or injure people

cancer   a serious illness caused by the uncontrolled division of abnormal cells

chromosomes   threads of DNA found in a cell nucleus that carry genetic information

cloning   making an exact copy of something so that the copy and the original have identical DNA

databases   sets of data or information stored in a computer system

embryo   an unborn baby up to eight weeks after fertilization of an egg

endangered species   any type of plant or animal that is in danger of extinction

environment   the surroundings or conditions in which a human, plant, or animal lives

famine   extreme shortage of food that may cause death from starvation

fetus   an unborn baby from nine weeks after fertilization of an egg up to birth

food chain   a series of organisms in which each depends on the next as a source of food

fossil record   all fossils, both discovered and yet to be discovered

generation   one stage in the history of a species or family, for example a grandparent, parent, or child

habitat   the natural home or surroundings of any living organism

hereditary   parts that are passed down from a parent to a child

Holocaust   the mass murder of Jews that took place under the German Nazis during World War II

laboratory   a place used for scientific experiments and research

life insurance   a financial plan made with an insurance company that pays out money when the holder of the plan dies

mammal   any warm-blooded creature with a spine and fur or hair, fed by milk from the female parent

microscope   a piece of scientific equipment that makes very small objects look hundreds or thousands of times bigger, so a scientist can see them clearly

molecule   a small particle

mutations   changes in the structure of genes that can be passed on to offspring

nutrients   substances that are needed to grow and live healthily

organisms   any living things

predators   creatures that seek out and kill other creatures as a source of food

proteins   chemical substances, made up of amino acids, using coded instructions in genes

reproduces   creates offspring of the same species

resistant   able to stop or stand up to something

species   a group of organisms with similar characteristics that can breed together to create offspring

traits   characteristics or features that can be passed on genetically

INDEX